Two Guys and a Dog Make a Family

By

Brian McNaught

Dedication – To all those who have created logical families, biological or otherwise, human or otherwise, to which they have given, and received, commitment, prioritized attention, thoughtfulness, generosity, kindness, open and honest communication, gratitude, good humor, forgiveness, and love.

The Way We Were

Two guys and a dog started for us in 1976, when I drove from Detroit, with my Irish Setter, Jeremy, and met my husband, Ray, in Boston. I was 28, he was 25, Jeremy was 2. I'm 71, Ray will be 68 on his next birthday, and our Labradoodle, Lincoln, will be 2 on New Year's Day.

When we met, Ray and I had no sense of what aging for us might be like. It wasn't even on our radar. Aging is what ones parents and grandparents do, along with old TV and movie stars. We were vigorous, happy dancers, warriors in the gay movement, both poor but ecstatic.

We cried 11 years later when we put Jeremy to sleep on Halloween, and buried him in our yard in Gloucester. We had stepped up in life, living in a mini-estate, furnished with some of the same treasures we had found in the rafters of antique shops, but adding to them such things as club chairs upholstered in high end designer fabrics.

Ray worked for Lehman Brothers, I was the Mayor of Boston's Liaison to the Gay Community, we hosted dinners in our home for people with AIDS in 1983, as well as for all of the gay Democratic luminaries in the state, and we purchased a yellow Lab puppy. Young Brit helped us continue to imagine ourselves as youthful, with walks in the woods, and thrown balls on the beach, but we were more preoccupied with the image of living well than we were aware and grateful for what we actually had.

It was so painful for us to put Brit down at 15, that Ray swore we'd never get another dog. By then, we had two homes, one in Provincetown and the other in New York, San Francisco, Naples, and then Ft. Lauderdale. We sold the Provincetown place after 16 years, and bought in the Adirondacks of New York. Thirteen years after Brit was buried in our yard in Provincetown, Ray relented and we brought Lincoln into our lives.

We have a lot of nice stuff north and south, and Lincoln is the first dog allowed to sit on it. He actually sits wherever he wants, which is often where I sit. He sees me coming and up on the sofa or bed he leaps, not in defiance but to get my attention and make me laugh.

Ray is retired, I'm semi-retired, and in our clearly aging bodies, we're very aware of how privileged we've been in our lives. For forty-three years, as our friends will attest, Ray and I have held hands at dinner, and expressed gratitude for what we had. When we first met, we prayed to God, then to Love, and then to the Universe. Raised Catholic, we'd probably be labeled today as Taoist. And I, at least, am back to using the word "God."

Ray hopes he dies before Lincoln, not because he hates life but because he loves Lincoln, and can't bear the thought of watching another dog look him in the eyes as he's given an injection, and then be buried on a piece of property we keep leaving.

In the beginning, as mentioned, in our young bodies, we were grateful for the bounty of our lives, starting with our mutual love, our close friends, the family members with whom we were speaking, recovery from alcohol addiction, world travel, successful careers, and princely living. Now our gratitude is about becoming aware that nothing that happens outside of the present moment has significance, including all of the aforementioned reasons for gratitude.

Ray now is significantly disabled by all the metal, wires, and battery packs in his back, all trying to relieve him of pain, but causing as much as they cured, if not more. We don't travel easily, nor dance, nor make love, the latter more to do with the medicinal drugs we take than the pain we're both in.

Where did 43 years go? But, here we are, two guys and a dog, now focussed on the final years of our lives, and of how possibly they will be our best. I like being my age, despite my awareness that I'll probably grieve the deaths of Lincoln and Ray, before others grieve mine.

Through Thick and Thin

 Unlike Lincoln, who immediately takes shotgun in the old, red, Mercedes convertible, Jeremy always jumped into the back of my red Opel station wagon. Perhaps, had it been a Mercedes, the Irish setter, that I had given to a previous boyfriend for Christmas, would have wanted to ride up front too.

 Maybe he stayed in the back of the Opel because it was easier for me to feed him there, mostly White Castle burgers and fries. I'd get a dozen burgers, and split them with him, the same way I give Lincoln Dairy Queen vanilla soft serve now. "One spoonful for you. One spoonful for me."

 Jeremy made the pilgrimage with me from Detroit's chapter of Dignity to Boston, where the national office was located. I was semi-famous enough for Ray to know who I was. In 1974, I went on a hunger strike to protest the sins of the Catholic Church against gay people. When that ended, the Church fired me as a columnist and reporter, so I became a columnist and reporter in the gay press. That notoriety might have scared many gay people from being seen with me in public, but not Ray. It's not all that uncommon, you know, for closeted gay people not wanting to be seen with gay "activists." When I was one of the only openly gay people in Boston City Hall in 1982, it was only a brave two guys who would have lunch with me. When Ray had a rainbow flag on his desk at Lehman Brothers, only one young woman identified herself to him, this despite him being a managing director of the firm. I used to laugh when I watched closeted gay friends run from the produce section of the grocery store when they saw me heading in for a hug.

The Irish setter didn't know "gay." He barked at Ray when my new roommate, and now husband of 43 years, climbed into the front seat of the Opel. But then the dog stopped, which told me that there was something in the vibrations of this handsome, strawberry blond man that appealed to both the dog and to me. Jeremy and I both counted on the kindness of this stranger to find our new home in Brookline, just over the Boston line, for the next eight years of our lives.

Poor Jeremy was our first dog, and as such, had the most strict, and clueless parents of any of the three dogs in our history. Oldest children will relate. We've learned in raising Lincoln, the spoiled Labradoodle, that any mistake the puppy makes is our fault, and not that of the dog. If the dog peed and pooped inside, we should have taken him out. If he chewed the table leg, we should have watched his behavior, and given him something else to chew. But, there were no such modern parenting methods with Jeremy. Whatever bad happened was always his fault. If he tipped over the kitchen garbage can while we were away, he was a bad boy. If he locked himself in the bathroom, it was his doing. He was loved deeply by us, but we had no dog owner training as twenty-year-olds, even having had dogs as children. I wish we could have a do-over with him. And, yet, we were perfect for each other, and the three of us were a tight family.

Jeremy had an opinion on everything, and readily gave it to everyone, whether they wanted to hear it or not, including to Elaine Noble, Lily Tomlin, Lisa Myers, Gerry Studds, Barney Frank, Neil Miller, Sr. Jeannine Gramick, Fr. Paul Stanley, Tomie dePaola, Stephen McCauley, and Gregory Maguire, among others. They all visited our third floor Brookline apartment, or our home in Gloucester, and all became aware of the Irish setter's voice. They also all loved him.

It was clear that Jeremy was my dog, although he and Ray had a love affair. But I was the alpha, and I made the rules, or lack thereof. While Lincoln gets no human food (except soft serve), Jeremy got whatever he wanted. It got to the point that he wouldn't eat his dinner without decent scraps, and I never was able to finish a whole bowl of ice cream without him pawing his way into my heart and dessert.

Our three dogs, Jeremy, Brit, and Lincoln, have collectively ridden in a large assortment of cars, and like children, have encountered us in various stages of canine awareness and maturity, as we drove the backroads of their lives. All three have been linked through the various ups and downs, and episodes of our lives – passion, separation, experimentation, addiction, recovery, addiction, suicide, recovery, gay politics, transgender awareness, wealth, lean years, notoriety, tears, screams, laughter, therapy, prayer, Catholicism, atheism, Buddhism, agnosticism, Taoism, visiting parents, dead parents, visiting young nephews and nieces, visits by the children of those nephews and nieces, 43 Valentine's Days, birthdays, Halloweens, Thanksgivings, Christmases, and Easters, hundreds of presents, dozens of temporary best friends, and not once did any of them complain. Well, that's not completely true. Jeremy barked, Brit walked away and curled up, and Lincoln sighs deeply.

If Jeremy or Brit were alive today, they would recognize our scent, but not our appearance. Lincoln knows that Ray walks with a cane, and that we both have gray hair. He's never seen us wrestle, or dance fast in the living room. Time passes. Dogs age and die, and so have and will we, but what a time we all have had, and hope to have together.

12

Memories Light the Corners of My Mind

Reel in the Closet, a 2015 documentary by Stu Maddox, compiled the home movies, dating back to the 1930s, of ordinary LGBTQ people, celebrating with their friends, none of whom knew they would one day be seen on the big screen, nor that their candid shots would become their legacy to us. LGBTQ museums today, such as the Stonewall National Museum in Ft. Lauderdale, covet such films and photos that help create a picture of what life was like for us all, prior to today. Do you have such films and photos? Ray and I do, of a period starting soon after the 1969 Stonewall riots to the present, a no less significant time, considering Elaine Noble, Anita Bryant, Harvey Milk, Marches on Washington, AIDS, Barney Frank, Don't Ask, Don't Tell, *Brokeback Mountain,* and Marriage Equality, just to cite a few reasons.

Do you remember when many of us were taking home movies? When I was a child, my parents held the camera up to their eye, and would direct us, "Smile. Say something." That was when you took your film to have it developed, and in turn got a yellow box with a reel of film inside. A few times a year, the family would sit together as Dad ran the projector, and Mom gave commentary. We kids would laugh, point at the screen, and say, "Who's that?" and "Look at you." It was a documentation of the McNaughts. All of my siblings have copies of the films.

Since Ray and I have been a couple, we've recorded everything with our cameras. When the photos came back in fat envelopes, we'd go through them together, pick out the ones we liked best, and insert them carefully, one by one, into beautiful, leather bound albums. We have at least two-dozen of them displayed up at the lodge on Tupper Lake. We also have stacks of discs that have been transferred from video camera cassettes. Now, of course, there's iPhones and iClouds. We create e-albums, and e-invite others to have access to the photos and videos. We also have Facebook, Instagram, Twitter and other social media outlets through which we can post a photo, series of photos, or video, to help family, friends, and strangers stay up on our lives. Most of us in the U.S. needn't fear social repercussions for posting these photos, unlike the gay and transgender people in the 1950s. They trusted that their friends would never show the photos or movies to anyone but "family."

I'm very glad that we have the photo albums and discs, but I rarely sit down to look, watch, and reminisce. I have fantasies of enjoying the discs, and slowly going through the photo albums, as I linger on my deathbed, long enough to complete the task. But, I don't get to choose when and how I die, and I hate to think I might miss the great pleasure of "lighting the corners of my mind," with memories of Ray, me, Jeremy, Brit, Lincoln, and our families and good friends.

When and why do you think we stop sitting alone, or together as couples, going through the photos, and watching the home movies of ourselves? When and why do you think we start back up, looking and watching them again? Wouldn't rekindling memories of our past enrich our relationships? The photos and the films prove that we existed, that we loved, that our lives had meaning. What happens, then, when they get tossed out a few years after our deaths because they took up too much space in a nephew or niece's basement? Do we vanish? Will anyone see firsthand proof of our full, beautiful lives?

I used to love it when Mom would guide us through the old photos of her family, telling us how our great uncle Frank used to be a flashy dresser and dancer in his day. We knew him only as the skinny old man with the whiskers who drank beer and smoked on the back porch of his sisters' home. Mom's grandfather was a ship's captain on the Great Lakes who drowned. (Dad joked he was drunk.) The stories created for us the sense of belonging to something bigger than just our immediate family. Some ancestors came from Ireland, others from Scotland. On one side of the family, or the other, we allegedly had relatives on the Mayflower. We learned that we were part of a living history of struggle, of succeeding, of glory, and of heartache, regardless of when we immigrated here.

So, too, are today and tomorrow's LGBTQ youth our children. They're part of your and my family, and they need us to explain who they're seeing in the photos. These young people belong to a bigger picture, to a living history that we helped create. While it's true that many young lesbian, gay, bisexual, transgender and queer youth currently don't seem to care much about their history, they, too, will grow older, and as they do, they'll be more interested in how they got to where they are now. So, please don't throw away the records of your lives. Don't let them get discarded by others who might not understand or care about the important stories they tell.

Before you donate them, though, sit comfortably alone, or with others, and slowly go through the albums and films so that you, too, might remember all of the struggles, the living, the grieving, the celebrating, and the loving of our lives. I promise myself that when I go north this summer, I'm going to sit alone, or with Ray, and look at the captured moments of our lives. I wish you could sit with me. I have so many wonderful stories to tell. And, so do you.

Keeping Them Together

When we found the silhouettes of the two guys and a dog, we knew nothing of Auguste Edouart. Ray and I were at an auction on the north shore of Boston, Jeremy, the Irish Setter, was at home, we both spotted the pair, and decided to join the bidding for each one, individually. We got both. That was many years ago. We paid a lot, but it turned out they were worth at least what we paid, and they haven't been apart since then. They've traveled to many states, and many homes, and the silhouetted dog came to represent different breeds, but they have always been within easy eye contact.

It's harder to keep a loving relationship together than it is a pair of rare pieces of art by the renowned 19th Century silhouette artist. A week ago, I learned of the divorce of two men whose beautiful, family and friends wedding I officiated on the beach of the Pines on Fire Island. The marriage was featured in *The New York Times* Sunday newspaper, in the Announcements that many gay men I know comb weekly. As you might imagine, I was shocked, saddened, and concerned for them. As it turned out, the sadness I experienced was for myself, as I had lost a significant piece of my romantic, hanging, love mobile, which was now out of balance.

The men in question are much younger than me, but they've been married for some time. Their e-mail announcement assured the recipients that they continued to love the other, but after much soul searching, discussion, and therapy they had decided together that life called them in different directions. These are mature, emotionally healthy guys who wanted their family and friends to be assured there was no "bad guy" in this decision.

I responded in part, "If you two beautiful souls are happy with your decision to divorce, I applaud the courage you brought forth to struggle together for reconciliation, and then acceptance that you are being called to grow in different ways. There is no failure here. True love of another can't be measured in years. The love that remains between you is taking a different form.

"Let gratitude, for the life you've shared, guide you as you deal with the messiness of separations. Things and money are meaningless. The question you will ask yourselves in the future won't be 'Did I get everything due me?' but rather 'Am I proud of the way I behaved?'

"You guys can't truly separate from one another. Your bodies can. Your souls can't. They are intertwined for eternity, just as mine is with you. We change each other. We learn from each other. We imprint ourselves in the souls of everyone we encounter. After the many years you shared life's experiences, trust that you will forever be a manifestation of that dance."

In our 43 years together, Ray and I have imagined separating many times, but it was always the result of a hurtful moment, not a true feeling that we shouldn't be together, or that life would be better without the other. We've had our moments when we each imagined what furnishings we'd take to decorate our new places, but those fantasies passed within a day or two, or a week, when we both came to realize that the fight was about nothing that couldn't be addressed with loving, open communication.

Sometimes our disenchantment from the other was the result of not being centered, of being tired, overwhelmed, jealous, hungry, confused, hurt, scared, feeling unappreciated, etc. Every loving couple has these moments, and some of these "moments" may require interventions and outside counseling. But, if you prioritize your relationship, and love, if not lust, prevails, it can endure most anything.

I look at my husband now, and I know he's not the same guy I moved in with in 1976. Though younger, he looks older than me. His chronic, severe back pain has shortened both his fuse and our walks. We haven't had sex in a long time because of the impact of his and my surgeries, and the meds we both take to deal with the pains and our prostates. But, when I look in his eyes, hold his hand, hear him laugh, watch him with children, see him care for Lincoln, and share with me his feelings, I know he is the soul with whom I still choose to dance.

Maybe when our bodies are both dead, the Auguste Edouart silhouettes of the two guys and the dog will be separated, but our souls are too intertwined for that to happen to us.

What Makes a Family?

Lincoln is asleep between Ray and me in bed. His head touches my leg because it assures his
connection. He's on his back, with his splayed legs across Ray's. My husband of 43 years is snoring softly. This is my family, my *real* family, two guys and a dog, all in love.

For a workshop exercise some years ago, I was given a page of drawn circles, the smallest being in the center, and others progressively larger around it. The task was to spontaneously place in the circles the names of others, in the order of their significance to us. The first circle was easy. It was Ray and Brit, our dog at the time. It never occurred to me to put my own name in there too. Why would I see myself as a significant person to myself? Learning to know, love, and take care of myself is a work in development.

After I put Ray and Brit in the center of the paper, it was an eye opener for me what names I put close to the little circle, and the names I put in the outermost spaces. In some cultures, I might have been kidnapped, and killed in shame, for not putting the names of my biological family in the closest possible circle. But they weren't there. Some didn't even make the page. The first names that came to my mind were those of people who loved and enjoyed me for who I am, and of those who I loved because they touched my soul with their innate goodness.

It seems strange to me that at funerals, biological family members are given the seats up front. The real friends of the deceased usually sit rows back asking each other, "Who's he?" "Oh, he's the brother who hasn't spoken to him for years." I've made it clear to Ray who I want allowed in to say "good-bye," and who I want blocked at the door to my hospital or bedroom. If I was in a king size bed, I'd want my favorite people to climb in and join Ray, Lincoln, and me.

Some people, such as myself, believe that when our bodies die, our souls enter a vibration of peace, love, and awareness. It's in that environment of complete acceptance and forgiveness for every soul that we see clearly all things, including how we didn't live our most recent human experience in sync with the Universe/God/Love. We then feel compelled to give it another try. This happens over and over until our souls are a complete and perfect representation of our divine nature.

Some people also believe, and I'm open to it, that we come back in the company of the same souls with whom we had our previous human experiences. In other words, Ray's and my souls have always been family, along with Jeremy's, Brit's, and Lincoln's. And Jeremy, Brit, and Lincoln might not have been dogs.

If I lost you a couple of paragraphs ago, it doesn't matter. Most of us who live in open cultures readily admit the difference between biological and logical families. Some of us celebrated the holidays with friends before making the trek to see family. That doesn't mean that we don't love our family, we just don't always like some of its members, or enjoy the dramas that play out each time we get together. I know there are families that are very tight, but it ought not be presumed that, even within a close family, everyone is enjoying themselves as much as the others.

I'm thinking about this a lot because Ray, Lincoln, and I are downsizing our possessions, (Yes, Lincoln too), which requires me placing in other's hands the things we don't feel the desire, or need, to keep. Although it's freeing to clear the decks of clutter, the question that disturbs me is, "Who should get the 'treasures' we're ready to pass on?" My first thoughts, as is true with our wills, are of family members, mostly nieces and nephews. But, why? Is there a right to family succession, even when you're of the mind that your closest souls don't share your blood, and that your blood members don't necessarily understand, much less share your soul? Maybe it's because most friends don't stay constants in our lives, but family is always in the picture. Their names and birthdays are tattooed across our conscious mind. And yet, in my soul migration, I'm not sure I want to have my next human experience in the company of all of my family members.

It's a conundrum to me. Why would I feel compelled to take a long, expensive trip to attend the funeral of a person who didn't make it into any of my circles? But, with people who were closest to my heart, I'd feel that at least I had a choice. Expectations make me uncomfortable. I want my heart and soul free of such clutter. I want my behavior to be in sync with my heart, and not with my head.

Lincoln has moved over so that I can now roll onto my side, and fall asleep, but I leave you with the recommendation of drawing the concentric circles, and see whose names go where. It might surprise you, and help clarify the members of your true family.

Shared Beliefs in the Unknown

Lincoln has been a Buddhist since he was a puppy. In his earliest romps around our lakefront property in the Adirondacks, he would stop, sit for long periods of time, and observe. In other words, he was in the moment, with his body and his mind in the same place, seeing, hearing, tasting, touching and smelling things for the first time. It's called "Beginner's Mind." You needn't be a puppy or baby to experience it.

Ray and I didn't embrace Buddhist and Taoist thought until much later in our lives. For the first thirty-plus years we were Roman Catholics. Both from families of seven, we each had sixteen years of parochial education. As youngsters, we both were trained as Altar Boy servers at Mass, memorizing all of the responses in Latin. We knew and said every prayer, speaking up clearly during "The Apostles Creed" that we believed in one God in three divine persons, Father, Son, and Holy Ghost.

There were advantages to sharing the same faith when we came together in a relationship in 1976. On Sundays, we walked together to Mass. Our friends were often gay Catholics. We read the same national, liberal Catholic newspaper, found interest in the same media reports on the Church, read the same books of inspiration, and then both left the Church with the same open wounds, anger, and rejection of Catholic doctrine.

Anita Bryant, Jerry Falwell, James Dobson, Ralph Reed, Pat Robertson, and other Evangelical Christian leaders get credit for alienating us from Christianity altogether, but so do the Popes, Cardinals, and Bishops who tried to drive non-celibate gay Catholics out of Church facilities. The biggest casualty in our messy divorce from Christianity was Jesus, an entity who, from childhood, inspired our fervent social activism with his recorded life and words of love and forgiveness. My 24-day hunger fast in

1974 was motivated by the Sermon on the Mount. But the obnoxious proselytizing by Fundamentalist Christians, with their "Honk if you love Jesus" bumper stickers, and their refusal to have funerals, and bury men with AIDS in their cemeteries, drove us away from the name, "Jesus." Not only did we no longer believe he was the one and only Son of God, we cringed when we heard his name. Nevertheless, we continued to draw strength from the echo of his teachings.

The same held true for the word "God." Ronald Regan, and the so-called Moral Majority, twisted the image of God into a grotesque, emotionally-abusive Father. The marriage of Right Wing Christians and the Republican Party made it impossible for Ray and me to separate "God" from intolerance. The spiritual craving that remained was initially satisfied by the Unitarian Church, that we believed to be welcoming to gay people. But even gathering with them sometimes felt emotionally unsafe, not because the majority of Unitarians weren't eager to have us think about spirituality with them, but because the small handful who were visibly unwelcoming made driving to church on Sunday unappealing.

Ray described himself as an atheist, I as an agnostic. We didn't stop seeking answers to our questions about life, death and the unknown, but not in the company of others. Several people, books, and other influences eventually led us to Buddhism, and to a teacher in Naples, FL, whose life reflected the teachings of the Buddha. Ray and I then came to see the *Tao te Ching* as the most useful daily guide for our hunger for union with our higher selves. For many years, we'd read aloud one of the 81 short lessons written 2,500 years ago. I now have an excellent sage, August Gold, in Ft. Lauderdale, who is a most credible manifestation of the lessons of the *Tao.*

And, a funny thing happened on the way to the *Tao.* I'm no longer offended by the word "God," which I now comfortably use along with the descriptive words, "Universe," " Love," and,

"Divine Life." I'm also good friends, again, with Jesus, which makes me very happy. There's nothIng quite like a reunion with the best friend from your youth. He's still not the sole Son of God, but he's a remarkably wise rabbi, and kind-hearted man. Actually, there are no spiritual words that now make me cringe. As the great teacher of comparative religions, Joseph Campbell, said, all the words mean the same thing.

Spirituality has guided Ray's and my life together, and, the lives of most people close to us, even if they're unable to articulate what it is they actually believe. Belief in the soul has helped me navigate choppy waters, to pay attention to the big picture, to esteem that which has lasting value.

It troubles me deeply that LGBTQ people have been so deeply wounded by many religious groups. It's actually outrageous that self-professed followers of any faith in the divine unifier would work to create divisions. That's why I'd like to be of some use to lesbian, gay, bisexual, transgender and queer people at the end of their lives, if, in fact, they are struggling with thoughts of what awaits them in their next manifestation. LGBTQ seniors, like those who died of complications related to AIDS, are in need of an army of people who will help them navigate a peaceful, meaningful death, and protect them from people who would have it otherwise, including family members.

Lincoln would be a great one to bring with me to the bedside of an LGBTQ person, as he's a very soothing presence. One can only feel joy and gratitude when petting this dog. But, he'd screw up my calling card, which I imagine could be, "If you're dyin', call Brian." However, it also could be, "If you're dyin', and thinkin', call Brian and Lincoln."

28

Sex – I Wish I Knew Then

One of the problems with wisdom can be, by the time you learn the important lesson, it's no longer relevant. Take "sex," for example. I have lots and lots of knowledge about sexuality. I'm even certified as a Sexuality Educator. I can talk with you about any aspect of sex and gender, but it wasn't always that way.

Growing up Roman Catholic, with strong Irish influence, my knowledge and understanding of the subject of sex was more than simply lacking, it was really harmful to me. I was so naïve and inexperienced that the psychiatrist I was required to see at age 19 as part of my acceptance as a novice with the Christian Brothers of Ireland, said, "You've had the sexual experiences of a twelve-year-old." I also had the sexual knowledge of a 12-year-old.

My first sexual experience with someone other than myself was with a very good-looking, hunky, freshman, who flirted with me in the dorm's TV room when I was a junior at Marquette. We'd sit for hours, not speaking, just the two of us. I finally initiated a quick verbal exchange, but he was the one who took control and action. Regrettable to this day, we fumbled awkwardly. I now had one sexual experience as a 20-year-old, but I was still sexually ignorant and repressed.

The second time I had gay sex was with a Catholic seminarian, and then another Catholic seminarian, and then an Episcopal priest. The Reverend and I played house, broke up, and then there was a Dignity crush. Finally, there was Ray, who was also a sexually ignorant, but far more experienced, Irish Catholic. My sex was all frottage (body-rubbing), non-penetrating, 100% vanilla. But, my sexual knowledge was far from that. I was an excellent trainer in a week-long, intensive, sexuality workshop at which we watched sexually explicit films, and had small group personal reflections on our own sexual history.

I knew all about G-spots, fisting, orgies, daisy-chains, muff-diving, and face fucking. I saw more vulvas than a gynecologist.

But, my sex with anyone was probably still 85% vanilla. And my sense of my sexual self was 10%.

After 30 years of explicit education, and frank, personal reflection on all components of sexuality, and many years and miles of educating others on the subject of LGBTQ people, I would now be considered sexually wise. But, for me, personally, it's too late. I can't get it up, and what's worse, I don't care.

While this isn't true for many seniors, as some of us get older, there's a greater chance of us taking meds for our prostate, neck, lower back, anxiety, insomnia, and depression. Those drugs take their toll on our libido, and on our ability to get an erection. Prostate cancer surgery has side effects such as retrograde (ejaculating inside your penis) orgasms, and peeing in Morse code. If you've been married 43 years, your husband can be a best friend, confidant, fellow traveler, but often not your sex partner. And, the more you don't have sex, the less interested you are, and the more difficult it is to perform. I'm sure if we added a hot young lover to the equation, I would rise to the occasion, but we've been there, done that, and we're not up to the emotional complications.

I'm 71, and I wouldn't mind feeling sexual desire again, but to what end? I take meds for mood and pain, I no longer masturbate, and I couldn't get an erection without the help of a pill. So, why bother?

In truth, what I want is my sexual youth back. I want a gay boyfriend in high school and in college. I want to experience all of my sex over again, but with more sophisticated sexual expertise. I want a mulligan. And, I imagine there are many people like me, just as there are many people who want a mulligan with their love lives. They wish they could go back, and undo bad decisions.

Now, I can hear the protestations from the 90-year-old gay men out there who are still getting it on, and gay male and lesbian long-term couples who in their 60s are Swingers, or have very satisfying sex together. The permeations of sex and gender are experienced in multitudes of ways. But, there are a lot of gay men, lesbians, bisexuals and queers, who don't think about sex, even if they talk about it non-stop with friends, teasing or boasting. They are happy sharing their lives with one special other, or experiencing it by themselves. It's enough to have someone with whom you see a movie, or take a river cruise on the Danube. People confuse sex with love. They are apples and oranges.

Many gay men are addicted to apples, and hunger for oranges. But many gay men who have the love represented by the orange, wish they had taken more bites out of the apple, and are jealous of those their age who still do. Eating a lot of apples, and eating a lot of oranges may make you knowledgeable, but it won't necessarily translate into sexual health and maturity.

We Never Know Who's Listening

Carson Kressley, gay television celebrity, initially known for his key role in the first *Queer Eye for the Straight Guy*, and now on Bravo in *Get a Room with Carson & Thom,* is coming to Ft. Lauderdale on February 22nd, as a personal favor, to present me with an award from the Stonewall National Museum. We've never met in person, but when I wrote Carson, and asked him if he'd come, he quickly responded that he'd be honored. Our lives intersected at an important time nearly forty years ago.

In 1983, when I served the Mayor of Boston, Kevin White, as his liaison to the gay and lesbian community, my younger brother, Tom, also gay, and also working for the Mayor, sent me a newspaper clipping that said Carson Kressley, when asked why he felt comfortable as a gay student at Gettysburg College, replied, "When I was a junior, they had Brian McNaught speak…" On a whim, I wrote him through his publicist, and got back a very meaningful note about my impact on his life. You just never know who's listening.

When Stonewall, here in Ft. Lauderdale, told me they were giving me their Legacy Award, I asked if they'd like me to see if Carson might come. I really look forward to meeting him face to face.

None of us knows how our words, actions, silence, or inaction impacts others. I've had the joy throughout my career of hearing how a talk, a book, or a video of mine had a positive impact on another person's life. I've never gotten a swelled head, but I have gotten a swelled heart from learning this. I don't make it about me. It actually has little to do with me. For me, for Carson, and for everyone else, when we positively impact others, we're channeling the truth, humor, joy, pride, strength, clarity, and kindness of the Universe. It's the light that seeks to shine through our window. And when we let it, it's our legacy to those around us, and to those who will live after us.

If I'm given time to speak after receiving the award for my work, it's my intention to talk about the legacy we've created together as a generation of lesbian, gay, bisexual, transgender, and queer people, and of our allies. After a talk at Notre Dame many years ago, I was approached by a Residence Advisor who told me that a gay student came out to him, and when he asked the student why he felt he could trust him with this very personal, mostly misunderstood information, the student said, "A couple of weeks ago, one of the R.A.s told an anti-gay joke, and you were the only one who didn't laugh." We never know who's listening.

Any person who was once heterosexually married with children, and came out, has been a full participant in this extraordinary global awareness that "Being gay is not what I do. It's who I am." Any transgender person who transitioned while married, and while on the job, has been a full participant in the legacy of normalizing the fluidity of gender, in identity and in expression.

Many years ago, most older people in our community mustered the courage to go into a gay bar, risking the loss of a job. We seniors marched in early Pride parades where people threw firecrackers at us. We dared to write letters to the editor, using our real name, to be photographed lying in the street with Act Up, to lobby our congressional representatives, pastors and rabbis, and union bosses, to hold the hand of a stranger with AIDS, to come out in the Armed Forces, to hang the rainbow flag from our front porches, and to put decals and bumper stickers on our cars.

We did this not in a welcoming environment because most straight and cis-gender people were uninformed, and frightened, and some dangerously hateful. Our vision of living whole, happy, safe lives in which we were valued by our family and friends, and protected by our government, was the evolutionary call of the Universe, and our rising to the occasion is our legacy to all future generations globally. Because, while we were writing, speaking, protesting, coming out, burying our dead, creating our quilt, and getting married, other people, young and old, gay, bisexual and straight, Catholic and Jew, rich and poor, black and white we're watching us, listening to us, and discussing us with others. And among them all, there were allies who stepped boldly forward on our behalf, and together, we changed the world forever. That's our legacy.

When my name and face were in newspapers and television news reports in Detroit in 1974, an envelope was left at the door of my home. It was from a 12-year-old boy down the street. The envelope had pictures of naked male statues, cut from a history book or encyclopedia. "I'm like you," the note read. Seeing me be an openly gay man gave him the courage, like Carson Kressley, to come out. You just never know who's listening.

Best Lessons Learned

A good friend has gone through weeks of excruciating chemotherapy treatments, without any guarantee of success. The regimen was so difficult, there was the possibility it would kill him. I don't know that I could agree to it. The thought of being continually nauseous makes me shudder.

The night before my recent birthday, as I hung onto the toilet for an hour and a half violently ill, I kept saying I wanted to die. I was totally depleted, trembling in cold, and my body and mind were out of control. I can't imagine possibly enduring that experience daily. But, you never know until you're in that situation.

My friend had the same physical nightmares I did, but he suffered nausea because of cancer. Mine was because I dragged longer than necessary on a joint. Luckily, it was an unusual occurrence for me, and one that I won't succumb to again. He doesn't have the choice. He can't say, "I won't do cancer again." Only, "I won't do the treatment again."

My mind's images as I crouched naked and sweating were so grey, empty, and scary, that I feared I would die. A strong voice inside me said, "You're better than this." I begged to live because I knew I had more work to do on myself, and in behalf of others. I shivered, and slept briefly on the cold floor.

Lincoln, our Labradoodle, was asleep on the bed of a guest downstairs. He heard me, came upstairs, stood anxiously outside the bathroom, and expressed his concern to Ray with a loud bark. Ray, in bed, suffered with me, listening in anguish to every pitiful sound, sometimes putting a pillow over his head, as he imagined the day when I might possibly be reacting to chemotherapy, rather than just strong grass.

I haven't had a drink in more than 25 years, and although I swore off pot too, it had never been a problem. Yet, there's always the fear that an occasional high from any source will trigger a slip with your poison of choice. If I had consistently good judgment in such matters, I wouldn't have ended up as ashamed and disappointed as I was with myself, as I begged for another day on the eve of my 71st birthday. But, I had hoped the grass would eliminate my need for a tranquilizer to ease sleep with my sciatica, and, I over-compensated knowingly.

It's the difficulties in our lives that teach us the most about ourselves, about life, and about what matters most. My life challenges have all been things that I could manage, and small compared to those of most others in the world, certainly to those of my good friend with cancer. I want to know from my friend, "What are your reasons for wanting to live under such conditions?" "What observations about accepting one's increased probability of early death do you have to share?" "How are you now a different person?"

Here's what I have to share from my own bad night. Slow down, and do things in moderation. You can always have seconds if you choose. If you have an addictive personality, don't screw around with your recovery. If you're having a bad experience, and it's your own fault, don't beat yourself up. Everyone makes mistakes. Forgive, but don't forget. Think about what happened, and consider the experiences of others, such as those worse off, and those who endured the effects of your mistake. Share your experiences, and the lessons learned with others so that they don't make your mistake, and so they learn from your reflections.

Also, be grateful. Be grateful for life, and the privileges you enjoy, and be very thankful for those who stand by you as you face life-altering challenges. None of us do much in life without love, and help, from others. My good friend has a husband who stood with him through every awful minute. So, too, do I. Single people have family and friends, and if not, they are always the recipients of the kindness of strangers. I am so very grateful for all of the love that guides and guards my precious life.

My heart embraces with more awareness today everyone who suffers, for whatever reason, the physically and emotionally debilitating experience of being so sick, they wish they were dead, but who actually want very much to live.

Such a Different Life, and Yet, the Same

We're north for the summer, in the forests, mountains, and lakes of the Adirondacks. We moved here after spending sixteen summers in Provincetown. We followed friends, who charmed us with sunset boat rides in a Chris Craft, shiny, wooden boat. Ray and I love the wilderness, most especially the wildlife. Not much could compare to the humpback whales and horsehead seals that often entered the harbor in front of our home in P-town, but, there's also nothing to compare to the crackle of logs in a fireplace, and the haunting call of the loon in a cove on our property. Our lives are very different from what they once were, and yet, very much the same. We're the same two guys and a dog, just in a different reality.

On my errands today, I cut through the back streets of the blue-collar neighborhoods of Tupper Lake, the former lumber town in which we live, seasonally. The magnificent spring symphony of blooming pink, purple, and white lilac, cherry trees, and the lowly but extraordinary yellow dandelions, reminded me so much of growing up in Michigan. I like the simplicity and dignity of these neighborhoods that petition year round to have their potholed roads repaved. Cracked cement walks head directly from the street to the front doors of the simple homes of these good people, who all are very family oriented. In Tupper Lake, everyone is related.

This is also Trump territory, though not as demonstratively conservative as some sections of the country. If it were so, we would leave, and warn others not to come. This is a new experience for us, but we manage, as other liberals do, by finding and clinging to likeminded people. Among the liberal groups here you'll find gay and straight people, well and under-educated, and those from all walks of life who share the same vision of America, and understanding of Scripture. What I've learned recently, from a program on NPR, is that 40 percent of why I'm a Democrat, and the wealthy garbage collector in town is a Trump Republican, is genetic. The liberals here don't see the world the way they do because they had different experiences growing up, but because their genetic make-up influences their perception of reality. We can't help ourselves. The other 60 percent is due to the influences of our environment and nurturing, over which we have more control. That same DNA, I suppose, can influence whether we choose to live in Provincetown or in Tupper Lake, or in both.

It's possible for researchers to pick out Republicans and Democrats based upon the way they process information. Tests where subjects were shown images, such as of a panda, a monkey, and a banana, and then asked to answer simple questions about the images, made it apparent who was who. So, you can have a liberal in Provincetown or Tupper Lake, but it's more likely the liberal's DNA would gravitate toward the tip of Cape Cod. Liberals are from Venus and Conservatives from Mars, but some of us, because of the 60 percent influences, are able to find peace and beauty in both.

Lincoln is neither a Republican nor a Democrat, but I can tell from his behavior that he is more likely to be a liberal. List quickly the characteristics of a liberal. Many of you know the story of Ferdinand the bull that refused to fight. That's my boy. Lincoln has never been in a fight, except when attacked, or competing with his brother to protect the seven-year-old boy they both feel duty bound to guard. Make love, not war. All we are saying is give peace a chance. Lincoln is like his two dads.

If it's true that 40 percent of the reason for our political views is guided by our DNA, is it possible for liberals and conservatives from either end of the spectrum, to truly understand what the other is saying? Many of us have had the experience of being completely perplexed by the political views of friends and family members. How can it be that two people raised in the same house can each be willing to die for opposing beliefs, or kill their siblings for opposing beliefs? Extreme, you say? Another American Civil War would put brother against brother, sister against sister. Are they each being pig-headed for no good reason, or do they passionately see the world differently because of their DNA, and other factors over which they had no control?

I was very successful in my corporate diversity work on LGBTQ+ issues because before each presentation, I prayed that a power greater than myself would channel welcoming love to everyone in the audience. My use of words, and choice of examples were not confrontational. So, we could be from different planets but nevertheless meet in a space station to talk. What do we talk about? The things we have in common – faith, love, family, whales and loons, beach sand, blooming apple trees, and potholes. And we, each side, must gently reframe the discussion on immigration, abortion, nationalism, and welfare to see where we can understand the other's perspective, and perhaps find common ground.

Because we live in a Democratic Republic, we get to vote. We also get to try to convince others to vote with us. But we shouldn't set ourselves up for disappointment when they just can't come to see things the same way we do. Whoever wins the vote gets to pack the Supreme Court with people who share their brainwaves. What is the relationship between the panda, the monkey, and the banana? Right answer. You're confirmed to serve for life.

Ray and I bounce back like you, and like those old standing clown figures from our youth, that you could punch back and watch them spring forward, again to left of center. We spend our time doing more than build fires and listen to the call of the loons. We try to use welcoming, loving language with conservatives, and be mindful of how we're talking about them when we're with liberals. We can complain all we want, but only they can decide whether their vote betrays their values of faith, love, and family. To change their mind wouldn't mean they were defying their

DNA. Rather, they'd be weighing which values they hold most dear.

Sometimes, no, oftentimes, we all need to sit quietly together, and enjoy listening to each other's responses to lilacs and life as we each see them.

A Gay Mr. Rogers

Community leader, and author, Eric Rofes, was the first person to refer to me as "a gay Mr. Rogers." It was in the mid-1980s, at a "roast" of Eric, prior to his departure from Boston to Los Angeles. I laughed with the others in the room, but was young enough to feel defensive, probably incorrectly imagining that he saw Mr. Rogers as effeminate, sexless, and wimpy, a man who wore red tennis shoes, and cardigan sweaters, knitted by his mother, and talked to pre-schoolers with hand puppets. I wanted to be appraised by my peers as a writer and speaker, a leader of the City's AIDS strategy, and, maybe as a masculine, attractive man, but not for my kindness. I wasn't effeminate, sexless, or wimpy, I thought. Why would he say that? With more thought over the years, I understood that he didn't think of me poorly, and I came to gratefully embrace the comparison when I heard it. Mr. Rogers was a very kind man. I'm a kind man. Kindness is a most worthy attribute. Besides, I now wear tennis shoes, cardigan sweaters, and have puppets on my hands to entertain our young grandnieces and grandnephews.

As it turns out, Mr. Rogers was bisexual, telling a friend that he found women and men equally attractive. He was heterosexually married, with children, but I can imagine that if he had grown into adulthood a decade or two later, he would have been in a gay marriage. Regardless of his sexuality, Fred Rogers, a Presbyterian minister, was a very gentle, thoughtful, giving man who was dedicated to enabling children to feel safe and valued. It was Mr. Rogers extraordinary generosity of spirit that deeply moved a Congressional panel, and secured from them several million dollars for children's public television.

I don't know why some children seem to be innately kind, and others, in the same family, might need to work at it with more effort. I was one of the lucky ones who, as a child, naturally looked for opportunities to be nice to people, including strangers. Such effortless, and personally-rewarding kindness, attracted the admiration of the nuns, the attention of the parish priest, and the appreciation of the parents of my young friends. It also attracted the attention of girls my age, but rarely other boys, whose approval I sought. I was seen by some boys my age as a "goodie two shoes," because of my politeness, and my secret desire to live in harmony with God. That's not to say I couldn't behave in an awful way, which I did, on occasion, to my younger siblings. But when my head and heart worked together, I chose kindness.

I had a caustic, quick wit growing up that I used to protect myself, and to entertain others. By my senior year in college, though, I realized that I had hurt the feelings of, or shamed, others with my so-called humor. I was more like Don Rickles than Danny Kaye, neither name of which resonates with you, unless you're over 65. One man's humor felt mean, and the other's felt nice. So, I learned to focus, before I opened my mouth, on how my comment might affect the feelings of others. My goal was to have everyone feel safe and valued, at least when they were with me, or within my reach of influence.

Mr. Rogers said, "One of the greatest gifts you can give anybody is the gift of your honest self." The key to the success of my 45 years as an educator on LGBTQA+ issues has been giving the reader, or member of my audience, my honest self. And, lucky for me, an important component of my honest self is kindness. My reputation grew as a messenger with whom everyone could feel safe and valued. Even those who came to my presentation to disrupt were handled with care. I have always said that, "The messenger *is* the message." If you're there to eliminate fear so that people can become educable, you have to be non-threatening. I was the polite, Irish Catholic who dressed and behaved well, who quickly, by his behavior, established his credentials as a caring man, and whose personal story made them cry and laugh with me. They wanted me to succeed because I was a tender, sexually unavailable, non-aggressive, very kind man, just like Mr. Rogers.

We need, as a culture, to value kindness in children, as well as in adults. We need to go out of our way to affirm kind behaviors in girls and boys. Parents, neighbors, teachers, coaches, and camp counselors need to call out kindness as a value they cherish and reward. If television and radio advertisements insisted on kindness in their copy and speech, and if news programs were honored for giving as much time to reporting on kind behaviors as they do to reporting on horrible behaviors, then maybe young men like me wouldn't feel defensive when someone compares them to Mr. Rogers, or to some other famous person who will always be remembered for their kindness.

Embrace your Mr. Rogers. It's a game changer on your spiritual trek.

"How do you deal with your anger?"

The monkey could have been any age. I was five. I had a small box of raisins in my left hand, and, in my right, a handful of raisins, extended to the bars of his cage. When the monkey grabbed the box, instead of those offered, we both started screaming in anger. Neither of us would let go of the box of raisins. They were mine, I yelled. My parents anxiously broke up the fight, but I have, forever since, angrily responded to injustice. "He had no right." I've also learned to let go, or suffer.

A few years later, when I was president of my all-boy, high school, senior class, I learned an important lesson about anger from a friend who was sitting in the bleachers in front of me. I had announced a mandatory, after school assembly of my 200 classmates to teach them our competitive, school Field Day routine. When I saw that less than half the class was there, I started complaining angrily about how hard I had worked on a program to help seniors win the day. Terry calmly counseled in a low voice, "But, *we're* here. Work with us." Why take your anger out on people who have done nothing to deserve it? Focus on what you can do positively with others.

When the Miami television station flew me in to debate the head of Anita Bryant's conversion program, I went to dinner with the allegedly former homosexual the night before. During our theological discussion, I learned that it upset him when he was challenged to be inclusive of women in his biblical references. The next day, knowing that my unfeigned "Mr. Rogers" demeanor might open hearts, I calmly stated my case on why homosexuality was part of God's plan. John, Anita's spokesperson, was asked to explain his theology. When he began with, "God made man," I interjected, "and woman." John lost his cool, his focus, and the Miami television audience. The lesson learned was that anger unnecessarily scares people. If you want to create bridges of understanding, don't express yourself in an angry way. If you can get your opponent to say things angrily, the audience will find the individual unlikeable.

In my Irish Catholic childhood, my dear, saintly mother, insisted on "Peace at any price," particularly at the dinner table, in the car on family vacations, and most certainly in public. When she got angry at one of us because of our misbehavior, she stepped back and called my father into the situation. When she got angry at my father, she either went to church to pray, or to the grocery store for a head of lettuce. We ate a lot of salad. The modeling I got there was to step back, and away, when you're too angry to express yourself peacefully.

Recently on Facebook, I posted successive descriptions of my daily encounters with conservatives, the first with two, very young Mormon or Baptist missionaries who rang our gate bell to see if I believed in the Bible, and to read a passage to me. The second was with two men the next day in the produce section of Publix, one wearing a red baseball cap that read "Trump and Jesus Forever." The other, when asked whether he'd like his male family members to grow up and behave like Donald Trump, bragging about "grabbing pussy," countered with the name, "Jussie Smollett."

The young missionaries were met with kindness, but a clear understanding that gay people, such as myself, didn't feel welcome in conservative Christian churches, despite the basic two themes of the Bible, "Love your neighbor as yourself," and "As you judge, so shall you be judged." It was a very hot day, so I offered them bottled water, but they politely declined and disappointedly moved on.

I left alone the old man with the offensive baseball cap message. People like him are unable to hear why their behavior is inappropriate. But, the other man, who said he was raised by liberal parents, had gay family members and friends, and gave me his card because he wanted me to buy his newly-created dog food, later that day received from me an e-mail in which I explained why his counterpoint reference to Jussie Smollett was very offensive to me as a gay man, and would be, I suggested, to his gay family members and friends if they were aware of what he said. He replied with an apology, and an invitation to get together to talk.

"How do you deal with your anger?" a Facebook friend asked me after reading the posts.

I get angry, the intensity of which depends upon how tired, hungry, and feeling overwhelmed I am. I can get angry at the behaviors of my husband, the dog, family and friends, Academy Award voters and recipients, the UPS driver, the person ahead of me in line who looks for the exact change, TV commentators, radio talk show hosts, and myself for forgetting I had something in a pan, simmering, but now burning on the stove.

Ray and I apologize quickly if we unskillfully express our anger. I'm also quick to apologize to anyone I feel should have been spoken to more kindly. I've learned to breathe, to step back, and to try to understand the other person's perspective.

Flashes of anger, particularly at minor injustices, are normal. Feeding anger with the reasons you have a right to be angry, does no one any good. Staying angry is, as is commonly said, like drinking poison hoping it kills the other person. Life is way too short and unpredictable to waste time with negative feelings that have detrimental effects on your entire body, and that of others.

There are many times, especially at this moment in history, with our instant daily awareness of the cruelty that is taking place all around us, when not being angry would indicate a withered heart. An unending battle against the threatening behaviors of others, either toward ourselves or toward other marginalized people, animals, or nature, must be uppermost in our lives if we have any sense of decency. The trick is to fight like hell against the behavior of others, and not against their malfunctioning souls. It's also to realize that anger is a useful weapon if handled with care. Nothing is achieved if we self-destruct in the name of love.

Anger must sometimes be released, like a box of raisins, in order to engage injustice another day. And, our anger must be controlled, sometimes by a trip to the grocery store for a head of lettuce, so that it doesn't permanently wound ourselves or others.

Laughter Gets Us Through It All

Ray has a wonderful laugh. He's the guy you're glad is in the theater audience watching a funny play or film. It's hysterical when he's on the plane with earphones listening to a movie. His laugh creates big smiles and chuckles for several rows. For forty-three years, his laughter has lifted my heart, and for forty-three years, it's been a primary objective of mine, no matter what the circumstances, to make him laugh. Although, we've learned, that making someone laugh who has just had a hernia operation is not necessarily a kindness.

I love to make Ray laugh. I can be pretty funny, and outrageous, and he loves my sense of humor. So, every day, from the moment we kiss "good morning," to the moment we kiss "good night," if a situation arises that strikes me as funny, I share it with Ray, sometimes with a quip, sometimes with the voices of different characters, sometimes dancing in front of the television, but, most often teasing him in front of others. He looks forward to it. The dogs have done their part too, Jeremy, Brit, and Lincoln. The Labradoodle knows he's funny when he runs around the house with my oh-so-sexy underwear in his mouth, tail wagging, as he waits to be chased. Everyone smiles when Lincoln rides around with me in the passenger seat of the old, red Mercedes convertible.

Laughter is great medicine for the body and the soul. It releases endorphins that actually help fight disease. Some groups of people find it easy to see the humor in life. The Irish and Jews can be non-stop hysterical. If you're in the hospital, and they ask you your faith, say "Jewish." The rabbi will make you laugh.

It heartens me of late to watch my husband begin to laugh on his own more easily, and more often. For many years, his mood has been heavier, less joyful, because of financial stress. We're rich by all measures, but our financial stability has been teetering since we loaned money to friends. Even that drama is something we can laugh about, but the joke takes a long set up.

Ray's lightened mood is the direct result of us, for the first time, working as a team to become more financially stable. That has included selling both homes. We've also sold most of our art and high-end antiques. We've moved into a smaller home, more suited to our age and needs. But please don't feel badly. We're actually happy, and excited about it. And, I've saved enough lifelong "treasures" that we don't feel wanting.

Financial security has been my soulmate's primary focus. He has kept the finances as his sole domain. His goal in our marriage is to have me be happy. I have the same goal as him, having me be happy. Kidding. My goal is having Ray be happy, but we each go about it differently. Anything I say in passing becomes his immediate objective to buy, and make real. Despite my constant assurance that I am happy, and need nothing, he nevertheless zeroes in on things he thinks will make me feel special and loved. For the past ten years, he has carried the weight of financial insecurity on his own back in shame, and in disappointment in himself. What changed for him was the realization that I was stepping in to make the decisions he knew needed to be made. A burden shared is a burden halved.

My primary objective in our marriage is to know that the love of my life will die with no regrets, a man fully fulfilled, and free from worry. With the time that has been made available with no work-related traveling, I'm focusing more and more attention on our final years together. I want Ray away from the desk where he has balanced credit card debt, paid bills, and worried about whether we'd have enough money to make it to the end. We will. Now, it's time to reconnect, play, and be light hearted.

Given the constant severe pain my spouse is in, as a result of back problems, and too much surgery, it's a marvel to me that he smiles and laughs as much as he does. Every time he looks at me, he smiles. And what a smile he has. It lights the room, and my soul.

All of us, regardless of our circumstances, need to smile and laugh more often. Even if we force ourselves to smile, it lifts our mood, and changes our focus. Our spouses want us to laugh, as do the people checking us out of the doctor's office or grocery store. Laughter is a common denominator that eliminates consciousness of class or power.

Have you ever laughed with a sick friend, or one who has just buried a loved one? They're grateful for the release from their prison of dread. They're exhausted by their pain and sorrow, and want to feel normal again, if even for just a brief moment. The same is true with those we love the most. They want to laugh, to smile, to feel light and joyful.

If you feel that you have no sense of humor, rent a funny movie, watch *The Marvelous Mrs. Maisel,* and make friends with people who make you laugh. I may get a business card made up that says, *"If You're Cryin', Call Brian,"* which should never get mixed in with my end-of-life spiritual doula cards, *"If You're Dyin', Call Brian."*

Moms, Dogs, and Dads

Color me jealous when I hear another gay man talk about his close friendship with his father. That wasn't in the cards for me. I have always blamed my father for our lack of closeness, because he clearly didn't want to be friends with his children. His generation believed "Father Knows Best." He was the father, and you obeyed.

My father had to have been as disappointed in me as I was in him, because I didn't give him what he wanted either, which was a son who did what he was told. I wasn't the rebel who had parties at the house in my parents' absence, but rather the one who questioned everything. My dad never got the satisfaction of ending the conversation with, "Because I said so." Even if I didn't win, I had the last word.

It embarrasses me now when I reflect on how critical of my father I was for many years, including how he ate, drank, drove, farted, belched, blew his nose, smelled, and spoke. That was then. This is now, and I, at times, eat, drive, fart, belch, blow my nose, smell and speak like my father when he was my age. Justice. As you judge, so shall you be judged. But, I am without children of my own, and my grand nieces and nephews have a friendship with me that make it less likely they'll be as mercilessly critical.

I was lucky in having a mother who wasn't afraid of losing respect by being friends with her offspring. My mom was spared my critical eye. Instead, I was protective of her. It sounds like a gay cliché, but I suspect most straight men had a similar relationship with their fathers and mothers. Among those straight men who feel they were close to their fathers are many guys who considered sharing sports and politics with their dad an indication of mutual intimacy. Most sons are protective of their mothers, often because they feel their fathers are not fully appreciative of them.

If I had a child that I nurtured from birth, providing them with everything they needed to learn, and grow into their own lives, I think it would be very difficult for me not to love them, and not to expect in return both respect and loving kindness. That's the rub. Children aren't obligated to respect or love, but only obey. I obeyed until I didn't, which is the first sign of individuality, something a parent should value. You hold them and keep them close until it's time for them to fly. Many leave the nest and don't look back. Others find reason to stay. Neither choice is an indication of friendship or of love.

It is the time of year for Mother's Day and Father's Day. I used to give my parents "Spiritual Bouquets" as an indication of my love. The less I felt love at the time, the more I pledged to attend Mass and say rosaries in their name. My dad got promises of more Masses than I have or intend to attend. When I had money, I bought cards and gifts. I always called, as did each of my siblings, all competing to see whose gift, card, or call got most mentioned by my parents to the others. Those Sundays pass unattended today, and would be unremarkable we're it not for the occasional e-mail from a niece or nephew thanking me for my presence in their life.

Our dog, Lincoln, has two dads, but there are no cards, no Spiritual Bouquets, no boxes of candy, or even long focused attention. But there is gratitude for providing him the love he needs to feel safe and protected, and there is no embarrassment of our appearance or behavior. We're totally accepted, obeyed, and appreciated, and have been by all of the dogs we've had.

My dad had a dog that followed him everywhere. My dad was never a disappointment to the dog, and the dog was my dad's best friend. The Universe, in its wisdom, makes dogs and cats available to both fathers and sons, and in them we all find the intimate relationship we missed having. I'm grateful to my dad's dog for giving him something his children couldn't.

The Changing Nature of Home

It's not true that the person who dies with the most toys wins. We're getting rid of most of our toys, and, I still feel as if I'm winning.

Nor is it necessarily true that you don't know what you've got 'til it's gone. Much of our "stuff" is going, but I have always appreciated what we have, I never took it for granted, and while I'm most grateful for the privilege of once owning it, I truly won't miss it.

Ray and I are disassembling what could be thought of as the "family" home. We've lived in many places, and our houses have always been thought of by close friends and relatives as the place to which they could return, and always know that if they needed something, we'd have it tucked away somewhere. "Need a tampon? We've got one."

Soon, our home will no longer be fully fortified for any need, nor will it be Auntie Mame's haven, overflowing with mysteriously beautiful artifacts. The exotic pieces from world travel have been shipped to the new, biggest house in the family, owned by a wonderful nephew and niece who happen to work on Wall Street. Antiques carefully culled from high-end and country auctions, and out-of-the-way curiosity shops, will now prompt compliments for their new owners, many comments coming from friends who also have small children, and are too busy on vacations to shop for treasures. As it turns out, we were our nephew and niece's personal shoppers.

We're lucky to have had the time, means, and shared good taste to create the palette of color and texture that have feathered our various nests of refuge for over 40 years. Guests always felt delightfully distracted, and pampered, as if at the Ritz, by the attention to detail, and the cultural feast easily seen from their beds. Despite our sobriety, the liquor and wine cupboards have been filled with the best a refined drinker could hope for. Holiday decorations were the talk of the clan, solid competition for Santa's Workshop. No longer. A handful of selected pieces have been set aside for future private celebrations of Thanksgiving, Christmas and Easter. But the extravaganza has been shipped out.

No room in the house has been spared. Every closet and dresser drawer has been culled of excess three or four times. We're cleaning house as if we're the survivors of our own deaths. If it doesn't sell, it's given away, some to family and friends, but most to household staff who load up their cars on cleaning and gardening day, with new treasures for families here, or for those back in their countries of origin.

This isn't the first downsizing of our possessions, nor will it be the last, but there won't be another until we're packed up for an assisted living facility, or retirement home. Even Lincoln, the two-year-old Labradoodle, is down from thirty to three toys. He wasn't involved in the decision-making, but we knew what to keep, and he hasn't missed what's gone. Others would laugh if they looked at what I call a housecleaning. Yes, we're down to furniture for two bedrooms, but our new home isn't sparsely or poorly decorated. We just no longer overwhelm visitors with all there is to look at. And we no longer have desk drawers or filing cabinets, so no more saving every card we give one another, or every finger-paint picture the grandnieces and nephews create.

Nothing will be missed, not a shirt, tie, pair of shoes, oil painting, or elevator. We're now glad for the simpler, single level living. I won't have room for the high chair, portable crib, three sets of dominoes for Mexican Train, Easter baskets and grass for a half-dozen visitors, enough cupcake, cake, and bake pans for a French bakery, wrapping paper for all occasions, ladders of all lengths, fertilizers for every soil and plant need, lightbulbs for all possible sockets, double and triple back ups for every spice, jam and syrup, stickers, colored paper, paints, crayons, markers of every color for visiting children, and enough changes of sheets and towels to accommodate ten.

It was money loaned and not repaid that put us in this crisis mode of purging property to cut expenses and generate income. There's a great story to tell if you like drama. It's been told so many times over a ten-year period that most friends and family have it committed to memory. I'm tired of telling and hearing the sad details. Enough. It doesn't matter. It is what it is. And, despite the physical toll it has taken on my beloved, it's really not such a bad thing, because it has forced us to do something very good for the soul, and for our future life together, that we wouldn't have willingly undertaken without necessity. We are cleaning up our "mess" before we die, and lessening that for which we have responsibility. We may enjoy this new freedom for as many as twenty years together.

Rich people who think they'll find happiness in "stuff" delude themselves, as do parents who think their family will fall apart, and they'll have no appeal to their children, if they sell the family home. We may not be able to accommodate more than one guest at a time now, but that shouldn't matter to those who really want to see us. We may find that our large number of friends change, but if we were loved for what we had to either enrich their lives or coffers, then best we know now while we still have time to meet people authentically attracted to our souls.

If I might share a couple of lessons learned from this, don't lend money. Give it away, but don't let anyone borrow it. You set yourself up for stress, and heartache, no matter how close you are. Secondly, don't wait until you have no choice about what things to get rid of. Place the beloved objects, for which you've been such great caretakers, into the hands of another, who will admire the beauty and historic value that you may have long since overlooked. Let your treasures, even if it's just a pretty lamp that belonged to Grandma, fill days with joy for someone much younger. By "cleansing," I'm not talking about recycling those things with chips, or tears, or lost parts that you no longer use. I mean the cherished china, favorite cuff links, and new blender.

Look through your files of every fabric you've ever used, of every Christmas card sent, every letter you've received from beloved family members, and enjoy the memories they bring back. Then, throw them away. Get rid of the CDs of every favorite Christmas movie. They're all available on cable. If you can live without it, live without it.

We are not diminished an iota, our lives have no less meaning, because we parted with the "stuff" of our lives. No one can take from us the experiences we've had, nor the lessons we've learned. Our identity doesn't come from our possessions, unless they possess us, in which case we're their possession.

For everything, there is a season, a time for everything to happen. As unsettling, and seemingly unnecessary as it might appear, when you're no longer having fun managing what's yours, let go, and move on.

Love in the Event of Death

While cleaning out the desk drawer, Ray came upon a love letter from me that was supposed to be opened by him on the occasion of my death. It was written in 1981, when I was 33, and it has been read twice by him, despite my good physical health. I wrote it not because I wanted the last word, which is not unlike me, but rather because I wanted him to be able to read again and again how deeply I loved him, and that I hoped he would love again. We had been together five years, and I left love notes under his pillow each time I left town, or tucked them into his suitcase when he traveled on business. But, we had no sense of what it would be like to be 71, and spouses for 43 years. We were young, vibrant lovers.

Why was I even thinking about death at that age? Because I grew up in a decade of assassinations of prominent people, and, I was a very visible, and easily accessed gay man who had lived with death threats since I was 26. Harvey Milk had been murdered in 1978, and the following year, Jerry Falwell blustered, and raised the hate thermometer, with his newly-formed Moral Majority. Ray was concerned every time I said "yes" to another speaking engagement on LGBTQ issues. Although I had no fear of death, I did want to comfort him should anything happen to me.

Today, I'll still write a similar love letter to again be tucked away in the desk, but I'd rather Ray's letter to me be about how to understand his management of our expenses, and about how to turn on the television. Ray has left me plenty of other reminders of his love for me.

No person should ever have to regret not communicating clearly and sufficiently how very much they love their spouse, children, parents, and friends. Nor should any person go to their death without knowing how others value them. Saying, "I love you," is so easy. Not having heard it said is so hard.

When you talk or write about death, people often ask you if everything is okay. The word "morbid" is used. I understood that sentiment when I was in my thirties, and was questioned by another thirty-year-old about a newspaper column on death, but, I'm old now, and thinking about my death, and what might happen to Ray, is not morbid. It's emotionally healthy.

The inevitability of one's death, and the death of all loved ones, is more feared than celebrated. If we truly believed in the soul, the kingdom within, Buddha nature, the manifestation of the Universe, soul migration, etc., then the death of the flesh would be embraced as a necessary step toward fully experiencing our true nature. It can be excruciatingly painful to let go of a loved one, but that is because we don't want our lives to change. We want tangible proof that the loved one is still there. That being said, I'd be an emotional mess if Ray, Lincoln, or the form of other cherished souls dies before I do. But, I'd have no regrets that they died without knowing my feelings, nor would I feel that my communication with them had ended.

Everyone reading this has been confronted with death, the most painful of all human experiences. And none of us believe that others truly understand the depth of our despair. Just because others have lost their beloved doesn't lessen our pain an iota. As time passes, and the wound is less sensitive, it helps to share stories with someone we think understands. But, we are nevertheless surrounded by constant reminders of what once was. Photos, clothes, the king size bed, routines, family, and friends, and maybe a love letter in the desk, keep us aware of our life shattering loss.

The other day, Ray said he thought I was more emotionally dependent on him than he was on me. I was shocked. I felt the exact opposite, that he would have a harder time than I would with the death of the other. He might be right, though. I haven't yet learned to be happy in my own company. But, from our earliest days forty-three years ago, I imagined myself as his emotional Border collie. His remark reminded me that even after all of our shared time and experiences, there's a great deal about Ray that's a mystery to me. I suppose the same is true for him with me. We have known patterns of behavior, but what is each deeply feeling? I don't expect to fully understand Ray until both of our deaths free our souls to dance together through eternity.

Many of us are in the final act of our lives. We can deny or embrace that reality. We can prepare ourselves, and our loved ones, for the event, by saying what needs to be said, getting our affairs in order, and our wishes known, or we can deny its inevitability, to our own regret, and to that of those we adore.

Thank You

You have many things to do with your time, and your time is limited and precious. Thank you for spending this time with me and my family. If you're interested in reading many of books, and watching my videos for free, go to www.brian-mcnaught.com.

My other books you might enjoy

A Disturbed Peace
On Being Gay
Gay Issues in the Workplace
Now That I'm Out, What Do I Do?
"Sex Camp"
"Are You Guys Brothers?"
The Lincoln Chronicles – Puppy Wisdom for Happy Living
Brian McNaught's Guide on LGBTQ+ Issues in the Workplace
Grog is a Frog Without Polliwogs
"What's 'Gay'?" Asked Mae

Made in the USA
Middletown, DE
24 October 2020